I'M A HOME OWNER. NOW WHAT?

A PORTABLE GUIDE TO ORGANIZING YOUR NEW HOME

KEEP TRACK OF MAINTENANCE, REMODELING, APPLIANCES, ELECTRONICS, & MORE

PETER PAUPER PRESS, INC.
WHITE PLAINS, NEW YORK

PETER PAUPER PRESS
Fine Books and Gifts Since 1928

Our Company

In 1928, at the age of twenty-two, Peter Beilenson began printing books on a small press in the basement of his parents' home in Larchmont, New York. Peter—and later, his wife, Edna—sought to create fine books that sold at "prices even a pauper could afford."

Today, still family owned and operated, Peter Pauper Press continues to honor our founders' legacy—and our customers' expectations—of beauty, quality, and value.

Images used under license from Shutterstock.com

Designed by Margaret Rubiano

Copyright © 2016
Peter Pauper Press, Inc.
202 Mamaroneck Avenue
White Plains, NY, 10601 USA
All rights reserved
ISBN 978-1-4413-2176-3
Printed in China

14 13 12 11 10 9

Visit us at www.peterpauper.com

I'M A HOME OWNER. NOW WHAT?

A PORTABLE GUIDE TO ORGANIZING YOUR NEW HOME

KEEP TRACK OF MAINTENANCE, REMODELING, APPLIANCES, ELECTRONICS, & MORE

WELCOME HOME!

Your home is your safe haven, your refuge, your port in a storm. Taking care of it requires attention, effort, money . . . and remembering what to do when, or when you did what. Here are fill-in lists and spaces for keeping track of home maintenance and improvements, when to change filters and smoke detector batteries, and all things domestic.

Regularly perform your own DIY inspections on foundation, roof, walls, garage, driveway, stairs, deck, fences, landscape plants, fireplaces and chimneys, attic, windows and doors, flooring, and the like—checking for such problems as cracks and leaks, missing shingles, peeling paint, rotted wood, and broken masonry, then record your observations and actions (if any) in the yellow "Inspection & Maintenance Logs" throughout.

There's no place like home!

MY HOME

Use the following pages to record basic information about your home, from your new address to your homeowner's insurance.

BASIC INFORMATION

Address ....

....

Zoning .... Style ....

Built .... Purchased ....

Sq. ft. .... Lot size ....

# of rooms .... # of bedrooms .... # of bathrooms ....

Tax I.D. number ....

Zoning considerations, easements, etc. ....

....

House History: Record details about the past owners of your house below.

OWNER	DATES LIVED IN	PURCHASE PRICE	NOTES

INSURANCE INFORMATION

Homeowner's insurance company: ....

Contact information: ....

Deductible: ....

Liability/damage limits: ....

....

Title insurance company: ....

Contact information: ....

MORTGAGE INFORMATION

Bank or mortgage lender ....

Date of transfer ....

Loan/account number ....

Interest rate/length of term ....

Contact information ....

Notes ....

....

....

....

HOME PURCHASE CONTACTS

Seller

Contact information

Realtor(s)

Contact information

Attorney(s)

Contact information

Home inspector

Contact information

Architect

Contact information

Engineer

Contact information

Surveyor

Contact information

Septic company

Contact information

Moving company

Contact information

Phone/Internet/Cable TV company

Contact information

Account number

Username and password

LOCAL CONTACTS

Town or village administrators

Contact information

Homeowner's Association

Contact information

Building and/or Zoning department

Contact information

Police

Contact information

Fire

Contact information

Trash removal service

Contact information

Recycling service

Contact information

ELECTRICAL

Electric company .... Account number ....

Website ....

Username/password ....

Box Type: ☐ Fuse ☐ Breaker Amperage: ....

Box location: ....

Main shut-off location: ....

BREAKER MAP			
CIRCUIT #	USE/AREA SERVED	CIRCUIT #	USE/AREA SERVED

WATER

Water source: Municipal   Well

Wastewater: Sewer   Septic

Main shut-off location: _____

MUNICIPAL WATER

Water company _____ Account # _____

Website _____

Username/password _____

WELL INFORMATION

Well pump type: Jet   Jet, in well   Submersible

Pump location _____

Storage tank location _____

Pressure switch location _____

Control box location (if any) _____

WATER HEATER INFORMATION

Location _____

Type _____ Fuel _____

Capacity (conventional tank) _____ Flow rate (tankless) _____

Brand/Model _____

Purchase date/from _____

Installed by _____

Warranty information _____

SEWER INFO

Sewer company _____ Account # _____

Website _____

Username/password _____

SEPTIC TANK INFORMATION

Septic service company _____

Contact information _____

Septic tank location _____

Capacity (in gal) _____ Date of installation _____

Dates pumped _____

_____

_____

_____

WATER SOFTENER INFORMATION

Softener location _____

Installed by _____ Date _____

Warranty information _____

WATER FILTER INFORMATION

Type _____

Location _____

Notes _____

_____

HEATING, VENTILATION, AND COOLING (HVAC)

HEATING

Type: ▢ Boiler ▢ Furnace   **Source:** ▢ Gas/Oil ▢ Electric

Make/Model ....

Purchase date/from ....

Furnace repair co. .... Contact info. ....

Furnace service record: ....

Heating fuel company .... Account number ....

Website .... Username/password ....

VENTILATION

Filter type .... Manufacturer ....

Model .... Change every .... months

Purchase date/from ....

COOLING

Manufacturer .... Model number ....

Filter type .... Coolant type ....

Recommended recharge frequency ....

Filters cleaned/replaced ....

Recharge date record: ....

Note: Record details of wall and window air conditioners in the Appliance Log in the Valuables section.

HOME EXTERIOR

Use the following pages to detail information about the exterior of your home, including notes concerning your roof, landscaping, deck, and other outdoor fixtures. Grid paper for mapping out your yard is in the back of this book.

PROFESSIONAL RESOURCES

Mason ....

Contact information ....

Roofer ....

Contact information ....

Gutter company ....

Contact information ....

Carpenter ....

Contact information ....

Paver/Bricklayer ....

Contact information ....

Landscaper ....

Contact information ....

Retailer ....

Contact information ....

FOUNDATION

Type of foundation ....

Installed on .... Installation cost ....

Installer contact ....

Insulated (y/n) .... Waterproofed (y/n) ....

BASEMENT DRAINAGE

Drain type .... # ....

Locations ....

Manufacturer ....

Installed on .... Cost ....

Installed by ....

Warranty information ....

Drain type .... # ....

Locations ....

Manufacturer ....

Installed on .... Cost ....

Installed by ....

Warranty information ....

Sump pump information:

Manufacturer ....

Installed by .... Installed on ....

Warranty information ....

INSPECTION & MAINTENANCE LOG

DATE   TASK   NOTES

ROOF

Roof dimensions:

Width

Depth

Square footage

Material

Cost of materials

Installed on   Installation cost

Installation company and contact information

Warranty details

Notes

Chimney:

Details and condition

Cap and flashing

Mason

Notes

INSPECTION & MAINTENANCE LOG

DATE	TASK	NOTES

GUTTERS/DOWNSPOUTS

Material ....

Feet of trough ....

Number of downspouts ....

Manufacturer ....

Style & color ....

Cost of materials ....

Installed on .... Installation cost ....

Gutter company and contact information ....

....

Warranty details ....

....

Gutter cleaning company and contact information ....

....

ROOF VENTS

VENT #	TYPE	LOCATION

INSPECTION & MAINTENANCE LOG

DATE   TASK   NOTES

HOME EXTERIOR

SIDING

Material

Square footage .... Cost ....

Manufacturer ....

Style & color ....

Installed on .... Installation cost ....

Installation company and contact information ....

....

Warranty details ....

....

Painting or Staining

Brand and color ....

Trim brand and color ....

Amount needed and cost ....

Purchased from .... Date ....

Contractor and contact information ....

....

Cost of work .... Date completed ....

Warranty details ....

Cleaning and Refinishing

Company ....

Description of work ....

Date .... Cost ....

INSPECTION & MAINTENANCE LOG

DATE	TASK	NOTES

GARAGE

INTERIOR INFORMATION

COVERING	SQ. FT.	MATERIAL/PAINT	PURCHASE INFO (COST/FROM)	INSTALLED /PAINTED (ON/BY/COST)
FLOOR				
WALLS				
CEILING				
TRIM				

EXTERIOR INFORMATION

Siding material

Square footage .... Cost

Manufacturer

Style & color

Installed on .... Installation cost

Installation company and contact information

Warranty details

Painting or Staining

Brand and color

Trim brand and color

Amount needed and cost

Notes

Purchased from .... Date ....

Contractor and contact information ....

....

Cost of work .... Date completed ....

Warranty details ....

WINDOW AND DOOR INFORMATION

	DESCRIPTION	PURCHASE INFO (COST/FROM)	INSTALLED (DATE/BY)
WINDOWS			
OVERHEAD DOOR			
SECONDARY DOOR			

Door opener information

Brand/Model .... Cost ....

Installed by .... On ....

Warranty details ....

INSPECTION & MAINTENANCE LOG

DATE	TASK	NOTES

DRIVEWAY

Square footage ....

Material ....

Installed on .... Installation cost ....

Installation company and contact information ....

....

Warranty details ....

....

Sealing company and contact information ....

....

Sealing date record ....

....

....

....

WALKWAYS

Square footage ....

Material ....

Installed on .... Installation cost ....

Installation company and contact information ....

....

Warranty details ....

....

STEPS

Square footage ....

Material ....

Installed on .... Installation cost ....

Installation company and contact information ....

....

Warranty details ....

....

INSPECTION & MAINTENANCE LOG

DATE	TASK	NOTES

DECK OR PORCH

Square footage

Material .... Cost

Manufacturer .... Source

Contractor and contact information

Cost of work .... Date completed

Warranty details

PAINTING OR STAINING

Brand and color

Amount needed and cost

Purchased from .... Date

Contractor and contact information

Cost of work .... Date completed

Warranty details

PATIO

Square footage

Material .... Cost

Manufacturer .... Source

Contractor and contact information ....

Cost of work .... Date completed ....

Warranty details ....

INSPECTION & MAINTENANCE LOG

DATE	TASK	NOTES

FENCES/OUTDOOR WALLS

FENCES

Linear feet .... Height ....

Material and style ....

Manufacturer .... Source ....

Gates ....

Contractor and contact information ....

....

Cost of work .... Date completed ....

Warranty details ....

....

Notes ....

PAINTING OR STAINING

Brand and color ....

Amount needed and cost ....

Purchased from .... Date ....

Contractor and contact information ....

....

Cost of work .... Date completed ....

Warranty details ....

....

Notes ....

GARDEN AND RETAINING WALLS

LOCATION	HEIGHT	TYPE/NOTES	DRAINAGE

Contractor information and other notes ....

....

....

....

INSPECTION & MAINTENANCE LOG

DATE   TASK   NOTES

OUTDOOR FIXTURES

SHED

Description and cost

Manufacturer   Source

Installed on   Installation cost

Contractor and contact information

Warranty details

GAZEBO

Description and cost

Manufacturer   Source

Installed on   Installation cost

Contractor and contact information

Warranty details

PLAY EQUIPMENT

Description and cost

Manufacturer   Source

Installed on   Installation cost

Contractor and contact information

Warranty details

INSPECTION & MAINTENANCE LOG

DATE	TASK	NOTES

PLANTS

Use the chart below to take note of what you've planted where.

PLANT TYPE	LOCATION	SOURCE/COST

DATE PLANTED	SIZE & QUANTITY	CARE INTRUCTIONS

HOME
INTERIOR

Use the following pages to detail information about the interior of your home, from the paint you use on your walls to the grand details of each room. Note that charts for listing all furniture, appliances, electronics, and valuables such as paintings are located in the next chapter, and grid paper for mapping out a floor plan of your house is located in the back of this book.

PROFESSIONAL RESOURCES

Painter

Contact information

Plumber

Contact information

Electrician

Contact information

Flooring service

Contact information

Chimney sweep

Contact information

Maid/housekeeping service

Contact information

Steam cleaning service

Contact information

Carpenter

Contact information

Insulation company

Contact information

Security provider

Contact information

Handyman

Contact information

Window company

Contact information

PROFESSIONAL RESOURCES

Lighting source

Contact information

Appliance retailer

Contact information

Equipment retailer

Contact information

Notes

SAFETY AND SECURITY

Security System ....

Manufacturer .... Contact # ....

Access code hint ....

Password hint ....

SMOKE ALARMS

LOCATION	MANUFACTURER	DATE INSTALLED	TEST DATE	BATTERY CHANGE

CARBON MONOXIDE DETECTORS

LOCATION	MANUFACTURER	DATE INSTALLED	TEST DATE	BATTERY CHANGE

FIRE EXTINGUISHERS

LOCATION	DATE ACQUIRED	PRESSURE CHECKED	LAST CHARGED

OUTLET MAP

	#	TYPES	LOCATIONS (NORTH, SOUTH, EAST, WEST)
LIVING			
KITCHEN			
DINING			
FAMILY			
BED 1			
BED 2			
BED 3			
SPARE			
BATH 1			
BATH 2			
BATH 3			
LAUNDRY			
ENTRY			
HALL/STAIRS			
HALL/STAIRS			
OTHER			
OTHER			

FIREPLACES AND CHIMNEYS

Paint/finish used on mantel

Brand, type, color, amount used ....

....

....

CLEANING & MAINTENANCE LOG

DATE	TASK	NOTES

Chimney cleaner and contact information ....

....

....

Record more chimney information on "Roof" page in previous section, Home Exterior.

ATTIC

BASIC INFORMATION

Rafter structure type ....

W/H of framing members .... Spacing ....

Dimension of floor joists .... Spacing of joists ....

ATTIC VENTILATION

Type ....

Description of vents ....

Exhaust fan make/model ....

Purchased from .... Date .... Cost ....

Installation company and contact information ....

....

Cost of work .... Date completed ....

Warranty details ....

....

INSPECTION & MAINTENANCE LOG

DATE	TASK	NOTES

INSULATION OF ATTIC RAFTERS

Type

Manufacturer

Purchased from .... Date

# of units .... Cost per unit .... Total cost

Thickness .... R-value

Type of vapor barrier

INSULATION OF ATTIC FLOOR

Type

Manufacturer

Purchased from .... Date

# of units .... Cost per unit .... Total cost

Thickness .... R-value

Type of vapor barrier

Notes

Installation company and contract information

Cost of work .... Date completed

Warranty details

INSULATION

INSULATION OF WALLS

Type

Manufacturer

Purchased from .... Date

# of units .... Cost per unit .... Total cost

Thickness .... R-value

Type of vapor barrier

OTHER INSULATION

Type

Manufacturer

Purchased from .... Date

# of units .... Cost per unit .... Total cost

Thickness .... R-value

Type of vapor barrier

    Installation company & contract information

    Cost of work .... Date completed

    Warranty details

NOTES

HOME INTERIOR

LIVING ROOM

WALLS

Description of walls (paint, paper, panel, etc.): ....
....

Total square footage of walls ....

Paint/covering used

Brand & color ....

Amount needed & cost ....

Purchased from .... Date ....

TRIM

Type of baseboard trim .... linear feet ....

Type of ceiling trim .... linear feet ....

Type of window trim .... linear feet ....

Type of door trim .... linear feet ....

Paint used

Brand & color...

Amount needed & cost..

Purchased from.. Date...................................

Contractor & contact details ....
....

Cost of work..Date completed..................

Warranty details ....

CEILING

Description of ceiling (paint, textured, etc.):

Total square footage of ceiling

Paint/covering used

Brand & color

Amount needed & cost

Purchased from   Date

FLOORING

Total square footage of floor

Description of flooring (wood, carpet, tile, etc.):

Covering used

Brand & color

Amount needed & cost

Purchased from   Date

Notes

Contractor & contact details

Cost of work   Date completed

Warranty details

WINDOWS AND DOORS

Type & material

Manufacturer & model

Size & number .... Cost

Purchased from .... Date

Notes

Installation company & contact information

Cost of work .... Date completed

Warranty details

WINDOW TREATMENTS

Description (blinds, curtains, etc.) & size

Brand & model

Color & number .... Cost

Purchased from .... Date

Notes

Installation company & contact information

Cost of work .... Date completed

Warranty details

LIGHT FIXTURES

Description (ceiling dome, recessed, free-standing, etc.)

Brand & model   Cost

Brand & model   Cost

Brand & model   Cost

Purchased from   Date

Notes on bulbs & control switches

Installation company & contact information

Cost of work   Date completed

Warranty details

INSPECTION & MAINTENANCE LOG

DATE	TASK	NOTES

KITCHEN

WALLS

Description of walls (paint, paper, panel, etc.): ....

....

Total square footage of walls ....

Paint/covering used

Brand & color ....

Amount needed & cost ....

Purchased from .... Date ....

TRIM

Type of baseboard trim .... linear feet ....

Type of ceiling trim .... linear feet ....

Type of window trim .... linear feet ....

Type of door trim.. linear feet ....

Paint used

Brand & color..

Amount needed & cost..

Purchased from.. Date..........................

    Contractor & contact details ....

    ....

    Cost of work.. Date completed..................

    Warranty details ....

CEILING

Description of ceiling (paint, textured, etc.): ....
....

Total square footage of ceiling ....

Paint/covering used

Brand & color...

Amount needed & cost...

Purchased from ....Date...................

FLOORING

Total square footage of floor ....

Description of flooring (wood, carpet, tile, etc.): ....
....

Covering used

Brand & color...

Amount needed & cost...

Purchased from.. Date...................

Notes ....
....

Contractor & contact details ....
....

Cost of work ....Date completed ....

Warranty details..

WINDOWS AND DOORS

Type & material

Manufacturer & model

Size & number   Cost

Purchased from   Date

Notes

    Installation company & contact information

    Cost of work   Date completed

    Warranty details

WINDOW TREATMENTS

Description (blinds, curtains, etc.) & size

Brand & model

Color & number   Cost

Purchased from   Date

Notes

    Installation company & contact information

    Cost of work   Date completed

    Warranty details

LIGHT FIXTURES

Description (ceiling dome, recessed, free-standing, etc.) ....

....

Brand & model.. Cost ....

Brand & model.. Cost ....

Brand & model.. Cost ....

Purchased from .... Date ....

Notes on bulbs & control switches ....

....

Installation company & contact information ....

....

Cost of work.. Date completed ....

Warranty details ....

COUNTERTOPS

Type & material ....

Manufacturer .... Cost ....

Purchased from............................... Date ....

Installation company & contact information ....

....

Cost of work................................... Date completed ....

Warranty details ....

CABINETS

Type & material ....

Manufacturer & model ....

Size & number... Cost ....

Purchased from.. Date ....

Installation company & contact information ....

....

Cost of work.. Date completed ....

Warranty details ....

Notes ....

....

....

....

....

....

....

....

....

....

....

Record details of appliances in the Appliance Log in the Valuables section.

INSPECTION & MAINTENANCE LOG

DATE	TASK	NOTES

DINING ROOM

WALLS

Description of walls (paint, paper, panel, etc.): ....

....

Total square footage of walls ....

Paint/covering used

Brand & color ....

Amount needed & cost ....

Purchased from .... Date ....

TRIM

Type of baseboard trim .... linear feet ....

Type of ceiling trim .... linear feet ....

Type of window trim .... linear feet ....

Type of door trim..................................... linear feet ....

Paint used

Brand & color...

Amount needed & cost..

Purchased from.. Date...............................

Contractor & contact details ....

....

Cost of work... Date completed...............

Warranty details ....

CEILING

Description of ceiling (paint, textured, etc.): ....

....

Total square footage of ceiling ....

Paint/covering used

Brand & color...

Amount needed & cost...

Purchased from .... Date........................

FLOORING

Total square footage of floor ....

Description of flooring (wood, carpet, tile, etc.): ....

....

Covering used

Brand & color...

Amount needed & cost...

Purchased from... Date........................

Notes ....

....

Contractor & contact details ....

....

Cost of work .... Date completed ....

Warranty details..

WINDOWS AND DOORS

Type & material ....

Manufacturer & model ....

Size & number.. Cost ....

Purchased from.. Date ....

Notes ....

Installation company & contact information ....

....

Cost of work... Date completed ....

Warranty details ....

WINDOW TREATMENTS

Description (blinds, curtains, etc.) & size ....

....

Brand & model ....

Color & number... Cost ....

Purchased from.. Date ....

Notes ....

Installation company & contact information ....

....

Cost of work... Date completed ....

Warranty details ....

LIGHT FIXTURES

Description (ceiling dome, recessed, free-standing, etc.) ....

....

Brand & model .... Cost ....

Brand & model .... Cost ....

Brand & model .... Cost ....

Purchased from .... Date ....

Notes on bulbs & control switches ....

....

Installation company & contact information ....

....

Cost of work... Date completed ....

Warranty details ....

INSPECTION & MAINTENANCE LOG

DATE	TASK	NOTES

FAMILY/REC ROOM

WALLS

Description of walls (paint, paper, panel, etc.): ....

....

Total square footage of walls ....

Paint/covering used

Brand & color ....

Amount needed & cost ....

Purchased from .... Date ....

TRIM

Type of baseboard trim .... linear feet ....

Type of ceiling trim .... linear feet ....

Type of window trim .... linear feet ....

Type of door trim .... linear feet ....

Paint used

Brand & color..

Amount needed & cost..

Purchased from................................. Date..

Contractor & contact details ....

....

Cost of work................................. Date completed....................

Warranty details ....

CEILING

Description of ceiling (paint, textured, etc.): ....

....

Total square footage of ceiling ....

Paint/covering used

Brand & color..

Amount needed & cost...

Purchased from.. Date..............................

FLOORING

Total square footage of floor ....

Description of flooring (wood, carpet, tile, etc.): ....

....

Covering used

Brand & color..

Amount needed & cost...

Purchased from.. Date..............................

Notes ....

....

Contractor & contact details ....

....

Cost of work .... Date completed ....

Warranty details..

WINDOWS AND DOORS

Type & material

Manufacturer & model

Size & number   Cost

Purchased from   Date

Notes

Installation company & contact information

Cost of work   Date completed

Warranty details

WINDOW TREATMENTS

Description (blinds, curtains, etc.) & size

Brand & model

Color & number   Cost

Purchased from   Date

Notes

Installation company & contact information

Cost of work   Date completed

Warranty details

LIGHT FIXTURES

Description (ceiling dome, recessed, free-standing, etc.) ....

....

....

Brand & model... Cost ....

Brand & model... Cost...

Brand & model... Cost ....

Purchased from... Date ....

Notes on bulbs & control switches ....

....

Installation company & contact information ....

....

Cost of work.. Date completed ....

Warranty details ....

INSPECTION & MAINTENANCE LOG

DATE	TASK	NOTES

BEDROOM 1

WALLS

Description of walls (paint, paper, panel, etc.): ....

....

Total square footage of walls ....

Paint/covering used

Brand & color ....

Amount needed & cost ....

Purchased from .... Date ....

TRIM

Type of baseboard trim .... linear feet ....

Type of ceiling trim .... linear feet ....

Type of window trim .... linear feet ....

Type of door trim... linear feet ....

Paint used

Brand & color..

Amount needed & cost..

Purchased from.. Date......................

Contractor & contact details ....

....

Cost of work... Date completed..............

Warranty details ....

CEILING

Description of cciling (paint, textured, etc.): ....

....

Total square footage of ceiling ....

Paint/covering used

Brand & color...

Amount needed & cost..

Purchased from .... Date..................................

FLOORING

Total square footage of floor ....

Description of flooring (wood, carpet, tile, etc.): ....

....

Covering used

Brand & color...

Amount needed & cost..

Purchased from .... Date..................................

Notes ....

....

Contractor & contact details ....

....

Cost of work .... Date completed ....

Warranty details...

WINDOWS AND DOORS

Type & material

Manufacturer & model

Size & number .... Cost

Purchased from .... Date

Notes

Installation company & contact information

Cost of work .... Date completed

Warranty details

WINDOW TREATMENTS

Description (blinds, curtains, etc.) & size

Brand & model

Color & number .... Cost

Purchased from .... Date

Notes

Installation company & contact information

Cost of work .... Date completed

Warranty details

LIGHT FIXTURES

Description (ceiling dome, recessed, free-standing, etc.) ....

....

....

Brand & model.. Cost ....

Brand & model.. Cost..

Brand & model.. Cost ....

Purchased from.................................. Date ....

Notes on bulbs & control switches ....

....

Installation company & contact information ....

....

Cost of work................................. Date completed ....

Warranty details ....

INSPECTION & MAINTENANCE LOG

DATE	TASK	NOTES

BEDROOM 2

WALLS

Description of walls (paint, paper, panel, etc.): ....
....

Total square footage of walls ....

Paint/covering used

Brand & color ....

Amount needed & cost ....

Purchased from .... Date ....

TRIM

Type of baseboard trim .... linear feet ....

Type of ceiling trim .... linear feet ....

Type of window trim .... linear feet ....

Type of door trim.. linear feet ....

Paint used

Brand & color...

Amount needed & cost..

Purchased from... Date......................................

Contractor & contact details ....
....

Cost of work.. Date completed............................

Warranty details ....

CEILING

Description of ceiling (paint, textured, etc.): ....

....

Total square footage of ceiling ....

Paint/covering used

Brand & color...

Amount needed & cost...

Purchased from ....Date...

FLOORING

Total square footage of floor ....

Description of flooring (wood, carpet, tile, etc.): ....

....

Covering used

Brand & color...

Amount needed & cost...

Purchased from ....Date...

Notes ....

....

Contractor & contact details ....

Cost of work .... Date completed ....

Warranty details...

WINDOWS AND DOORS

Type & material

Manufacturer & model

Size & number   Cost

Purchased from   Date

Notes

Installation company & contact information

Cost of work   Date completed

Warranty details

WINDOW TREATMENTS

Description (blinds, curtains, etc.) & size

Brand & model

Color & number   Cost

Purchased from   Date

Notes

Installation company & contact information

Cost of work   Date completed

Warranty details

LIGHT FIXTURES

Description (ceiling dome, recessed, free-standing, etc.) ....

....

....

Brand & model.. Cost ....

Brand & model.. Cost.................................

Brand & model.. Cost ....

Purchased from... Date ....

Notes on bulbs & control switches ....

....

Installation company & contact information ....

....

Cost of work.. Date completed ....

Warranty details ....

INSPECTION & MAINTENANCE LOG

DATE	TASK	NOTES

BEDROOM 3

WALLS

Description of walls (paint, paper, panel, etc.): ....

....

Total square footage of walls ....

Paint/covering used

Brand & color ....

Amount needed & cost ....

Purchased from .... Date ....

TRIM

Type of baseboard trim .... linear feet ....

Type of ceiling trim .... linear feet ....

Type of window trim .... linear feet ....

Type of door trim... linear feet ....

Paint used

Brand & color..

Amount needed & cost...

Purchased from.. Date...........................

Contractor & contact details ....

....

Cost of work... Date completed...............

Warranty details ....

CEILING

Description of cciling (paint, textured, etc.): ....

....

Total square footage of ceiling ....

Paint/covering used

Brand & color...

Amount needed & cost...

Purchased from .... Date................................

FLOORING

Total square footage of floor ....

Description of flooring (wood, carpet, tile, etc.): ....

....

Covering used

Brand & color...

Amount needed & cost...

Purchased from .... Date....................................

Notes ....

....

Contractor & contact details ....

....

Cost of work .... Date completed ....

Warranty details...

WINDOWS AND DOORS

Type & material

Manufacturer & model

Size & number   Cost

Purchased from   Date

Notes

Installation company & contact information

Cost of work   Date completed

Warranty details

WINDOW TREATMENTS

Description (blinds, curtains, etc.) & size

Brand & model

Color & number   Cost

Purchased from   Date

Notes

Installation company & contact information

Cost of work   Date completed

Warranty details

LIGHT FIXTURES

Description (ceiling dome, recessed, free-standing, etc.) ....

....

....

Brand & model .... Cost ....

Brand & model .... Cost ....

Brand & model .... Cost ....

Purchased from .... Date ....

Notes on bulbs & control switches ....

....

Installation company & contact information ....

....

Cost of work .... Date completed ....

Warranty details ....

INSPECTION & MAINTENANCE LOG

DATE	TASK	NOTES

BEDROOM/SPARE ROOM

WALLS

Description of walls (paint, paper, panel, etc.): ....
....

Total square footage of walls ....

Paint/covering used

Brand & color ....

Amount needed & cost ....

Purchased from .... Date ....

TRIM

Type of baseboard trim .... linear feet ....

Type of ceiling trim .... linear feet ....

Type of window trim .... linear feet ....

Type of door trim.................................... linear feet ....

Paint used

Brand & color..

Amount needed & cost..

Purchased from................................ Date...............................

Contractor & contact details ....
....

Cost of work.. Date completed...............

Warranty details ....

CEILING

Description of ceiling (paint, textured, etc.): ....

....

Total square footage of ceiling ....

Paint/covering used

Brand & color..

Amount needed & cost...

Purchased from .... Date.....................

FLOORING

Total square footage of floor ....

Description of flooring (wood, carpet, tile, etc.): ....

....

Covering used

Brand & color..

Amount needed & cost...

Purchased from .... Date.....................

Notes ....

....

Contractor & contact details ....

....

Cost of work .... Date completed ....

Warranty details...

WINDOWS AND DOORS

Type & material

Manufacturer & model

Size & number................................ Cost

Purchased from................................ Date

Notes

Installation company & contact information

Cost of work................................ Date completed

Warranty details

WINDOW TREATMENTS

Description (blinds, curtains, etc.) & size

Brand & model

Color & number................................ Cost

Purchased from................................ Date

Notes

Installation company & contact information

Cost of work................................ Date completed

Warranty details

LIGHT FIXTURES

Description (ceiling dome, recessed, free-standing, etc.)

Brand & model .... Cost ....

Brand & model .... Cost ....

Brand & model .... Cost ....

Purchased from .... Date ....

Notes on bulbs & control switches

Installation company & contact information

Cost of work .... Date completed ....

Warranty details

INSPECTION & MAINTENANCE LOG

DATE	TASK	NOTES

BATHROOM 1

WALLS

Description of walls (paint, paper, panel, etc.): ....

....

Total square footage of walls ....

Paint/covering used

Brand & color ....

Amount needed & cost ....

Purchased from .... Date ....

TRIM

Type of baseboard trim .... linear feet ....

Type of ceiling trim .... linear feet ....

Type of window trim .... linear feet ....

Type of door trim... linear feet ....

Paint used

Brand & color...

Amount needed & cost..

Purchased from... Date...................................

Contractor & contact details ....

....

Cost of work... Date completed..................

Warranty details ....

CEILING

Description of ceiling (paint, textured, etc.): ....

....

Total square footage of ceiling ....

Paint/covering used

Brand & color...

Amount needed & cost..

Purchased from.. Date....................................

FLOORING

Total square footage of floor ....

Description of flooring (wood, carpet, tile, etc.): ....

....

Covering used

Brand & color...

Amount needed & cost..

Purchased from.. Date....................................

Notes ....

....

Contractor & contact details ....

....

Cost of work .... Date completed ....

Warranty details..

WINDOWS AND DOORS

Type & material

Manufacturer & model

Size & number   Cost

Purchased from   Date

Notes

Installation company & contact information

Cost of work   Date completed

Warranty details

WINDOW TREATMENTS

Description (blinds, curtains, etc.) & size

Brand & model

Color & number   Cost

Purchased from   Date

Notes

Installation company & contact information

Cost of work   Date completed

Warranty details

LIGHT FIXTURES

Description (ceiling dome, recessed, free-standing, etc.) ....

....

....

Brand & model... Cost ....

Brand & model... Cost ....

Brand & model... Cost ....

Purchased from.. Date ....

Notes on bulbs & control switches ....

....

Installation company & contact information ....

....

Cost of work.. Date completed ....

Warranty details ....

Notes ....

....

....

....

....

....

FIXTURE LIST

	BRAND/MODEL	PURCHASE INFO (COST/FROM)	INSTALLED (DATE/BY)
SINK			
TUB			
SHOWER			
TOILET			
TOWEL RACK			
TOILET PAPER RACK			
CABINETS			

Notes

INSPECTION & MAINTENANCE LOG

DATE	TASK	NOTES

BATHROOM 2

WALLS

Description of walls (paint, paper, panel, etc.): ....

....

Total square footage of walls ....

Paint/covering used

Brand & color ....

Amount needed & cost ....

Purchased from .... Date ....

TRIM

Type of baseboard trim .... linear feet ....

Type of ceiling trim .... linear feet ....

Type of window trim .... linear feet ....

Type of door trim................................ linear feet ....

Paint used

Brand & color..

Amount needed & cost..

Purchased from................................ Date........................

Contractor & contact details ....

....

Cost of work................................ Date completed..............

Warranty details ....

CEILING

Description of ceiling (paint, textured, etc.): ....

....

Total square footage of ceiling ....

Paint/covering used

Brand & color...

Amount needed & cost..

Purchased from .... Date..............................

FLOORING

Total square footage of floor ....

Description of flooring (wood, carpet, tile, etc.): ....

....

Covering used

Brand & color...

Amount needed & cost..

Purchased from .... Date..............................

Notes ....

....

Contractor & contact details ....

....

Cost of work .... Date completed ....

Warranty details..

WINDOWS AND DOORS

Type & material

Manufacturer & model

Size & number   Cost

Purchased from   Date

Notes

Installation company & contact information

Cost of work   Date completed

Warranty details

WINDOW TREATMENTS

Description (blinds, curtains, etc.) & size

Brand & model

Color & number   Cost

Purchased from   Date

Notes

Installation company & contact information

Cost of work   Date completed

Warranty details

LIGHT FIXTURES

Description (ceiling dome, recessed, free-standing, etc.) ....

....

....

Brand & model..Cost ....

Brand & model..Cost.......................

Brand & model..Cost ....

Purchased from...Date ....

Notes on bulbs & control switches ....

....

Installation company & contact information ....

....

Cost of work...Date completed ....

Warranty details ....

Notes ....

....

....

....

....

....

....

FIXTURE LIST

	BRAND/MODEL	PURCHASE INFO (COST/FROM)	INSTALLED (DATE/BY)
SINK			
TUB			
SHOWER			
TOILET			
TOWEL RACK			
TOILET PAPER RACK			
CABINETS			

Notes

INSPECTION & MAINTENANCE LOG

DATE	TASK	NOTES

BATHROOM 3/HALF-BATHROOM

WALLS

Description of walls (paint, paper, panel, etc.): ....
....

Total square footage of walls ....

Paint/covering used

Brand & color ....

Amount needed & cost ....

Purchased from .... Date ....

TRIM

Type of baseboard trim .... linear feet ....

Type of ceiling trim .... linear feet ....

Type of window trim .... linear feet ....

Type of door trim.................................... linear feet ....

Paint used

Brand & color...

Amount needed & cost..

Purchased from .... Date...............................

Contractor & contact details ....
....

Cost of work.............................. Date completed...........................

Warranty details ....

CEILING

Description of ceiling (paint, textured, etc.): ....

....

Total square footage of ceiling ....

Paint/covering used

Brand & color ....

Amount needed & cost ....

Purchased from .... Date ....

FLOORING

Total square footage of floor ....

Description of flooring (wood, carpet, tile, etc.): ....

....

Covering used

Brand & color ....

Amount needed & cost ....

Purchased from .... Date ....

Notes ....

....

Contractor & contact details ....

....

Cost of work .... Date completed ....

Warranty details ....

WINDOWS AND DOORS

Type & material ....

Manufacturer & model ....

Size & number .... Cost ....

Purchased from .... Date ....

Notes ....

Installation company & contact information ....
....

Cost of work .... Date completed ....

Warranty details ....

WINDOW TREATMENTS

Description (blinds, curtains, etc.) & size ....
....

Brand & model ....

Color & number .... Cost ....

Purchased from .... Date ....

Notes ....

Installation company & contact information ....
....

Cost of work .... Date completed ....

Warranty details ....

LIGHT FIXTURES

Description (ceiling dome, recessed, free-standing, etc.) ....

....

....

Brand & model.. Cost ....

Brand & model.. Cost..

Brand & model.. Cost ....

Purchased from.. Date ....

Notes on bulbs & control switches ....

....

Installation company & contact information ....

....

Cost of work.. Date completed ....

Warranty details ....

Notes ....

....

....

....

....

....

....

FIXTURE LIST

	BRAND/MODEL	PURCHASE INFO (COST/FROM)	INSTALLED (DATE/BY)
SINK			
TUB			
SHOWER			
TOILET			
TOWEL RACK			
TOILET PAPER RACK			
CABINETS			

Notes

INSPECTION & MAINTENANCE LOG

DATE	TASK	NOTES

LAUNDRY ROOM

WALLS AND CEILING

Description of walls (paint, paper, panel, etc.): ....

....

Total square footage of walls and ceiling ....

Paint/covering used

Brand & color ....

Amount needed & cost ....

Purchased from .... Date ....

TRIM

Type of baseboard trim .... linear feet ....

Type of ceiling trim .... linear feet ....

Type of window trim .... linear feet ....

Type of door trim.. linear feet ....

Paint used

Brand & color..

Amount needed & cost..

Purchased from.. Date.............................

Contractor & contact details ....

....

Cost of work.. Date completed...............

Warranty details ....

FIXTURE LIST

	BRAND/MODEL	PURCHASE INFO (COST/FROM)	INSTALLED (DATE/BY)
SINK			
COUNTERTOP			
CABINET			
LIGHTS			

FLOORING

Notes on flooring ....

....

....

INSPECTION & MAINTENANCE LOG

DATE	TASK	NOTES

BASEMENT/CELLAR

WALLS

Description of walls (paint, paper, panel, etc.):

Total square footage of walls

Paint/covering used

Brand & color

Amount needed & cost

Purchased from   Date

TRIM

Type of baseboard trim   linear feet

Type of ceiling trim   linear feet

Type of window trim   linear feet

Type of door trim   linear feet

Paint used

Brand & color

Amount needed & cost

Purchased from   Date

Contractor & contact details

Cost of work   Date completed

Warranty details

CEILING

Description of ceiling (paint, textured, etc.):

Total square footage of ceiling

Paint/covering used

Brand & color

Amount needed & cost

Purchased from   Date

FLOORING

Total square footage of floor

Description of flooring (wood, carpet, tile, etc.):

Covering used

Brand & color

Amount needed & cost

Purchased from   Date

Notes

Contractor & contact details

Cost of work   Date completed

Warranty details

WINDOWS AND DOORS

Type & material

Manufacturer & model

Size & number   Cost

Purchased from   Date

Notes

Installation company & contact information

Cost of work   Date completed

Warranty details

WINDOW TREATMENTS

Description (blinds, curtains, etc.) & size

Brand & model

Color & number   Cost

Purchased from   Date

Notes

Installation company & contact information

Cost of work   Date completed

Warranty details

LIGHT FIXTURES

Description (ceiling dome, recessed, free-standing, etc.) ....

....

....

Brand & model.. Cost ....

Brand & model.. Cost ....

Brand & model.. Cost ....

Purchased from.. Date ....

Notes on bulbs & control switches ....

....

Installation company & contact information ....

....

Cost of work.. Date completed ....

Warranty details..

INSPECTION & MAINTENANCE LOG

DATE	TASK	NOTES

FRONT/BACK ENTRY

WALLS

Description of walls (paint, paper, panel, etc.):

Total square footage of walls

Paint/covering used

Brand & color

Amount needed & cost

Purchased from   Date

TRIM

Type of baseboard trim   linear feet

Type of ceiling trim   linear feet

Type of window trim   linear feet

Type of door trim   linear feet

Paint used

Brand & color

Amount needed & cost

Purchased from   Date

Contractor & contact details

Cost of work   Date completed

Warranty details

CEILING

Description of ceiling (paint, textured, etc.): ....

....

Total square footage of ceiling ....

Paint/covering used

Brand & color ....

Amount needed & cost ....

Purchased from .... Date ....

FLOORING

Total square footage of floor ....

Description of flooring (wood, carpet, tile, etc.): ....

....

Covering used

Brand & color ....

Amount needed & cost ....

Purchased from .... Date ....

Notes ....

....

Contractor & contact details ....

Cost of work .... Date completed ....

Warranty details ....

WINDOWS AND DOORS

Type & material ....

Manufacturer & model ....

Size & number.. Cost ....

Purchased from.. Date ....

Notes ....

Installation company & contact information ....

....

Cost of work.. Date completed ....

Warranty details ....

WINDOW TREATMENTS

Description (blinds, curtains, etc.) & size ....

....

Brand & model ....

Color & number.. Cost ....

Purchased from.. Date ....

Notes ....

Installation company & contact information ....

....

Cost of work.. Date completed ....

Warranty details ....

LIGHT FIXTURES

Description (ceiling dome, recessed, free-standing, etc.) ....

....

Brand & model .... Cost ....

Brand & model .... Cost ....

Brand & model .... Cost ....

Purchased from .... Date ....

Notes on bulbs & control switches ....

....

Installation company & contact information ....

....

Cost of work .... Date completed ....

Warranty details ....

INSPECTION & MAINTENANCE LOG

DATE	TASK	NOTES

HALL/STAIRS 1

WALLS

Description of walls (paint, paper, panel, etc.):

Total square footage of walls

Paint/covering used

Brand & color

Amount needed & cost

Purchased from   Date

TRIM

Type of baseboard trim   linear feet

Type of ceiling trim   linear feet

Type of window trim   linear feet

Type of door trim   linear feet

Paint used

Brand & color

Amount needed & cost

Purchased from   Date

Contractor & contact details

Cost of work   Date completed

Warranty details

BANISTER AND STAIRS

Details and Notes

INSPECTION & MAINTENANCE LOG

DATE	TASK	NOTES

HALL/STAIRS 2

WALLS

Description of walls (paint, paper, panel, etc.):

Total square footage of walls

Paint/covering used

Brand & color

Amount needed & cost

Purchased from .... Date

TRIM

Type of baseboard trim .... linear feet

Type of ceiling trim .... linear feet

Type of window trim .... linear feet

Type of door trim.. linear feet

Paint used

Brand & color

Amount needed & cost

Purchased from .... Date

Contractor & contact details

Cost of work .... Date completed

Warranty details

BANISTER AND STAIRS

Details and Notes

INSPECTION & MAINTENANCE LOG

DATE	TASK	NOTES

OTHER ROOM 1

WALLS

Description of walls (paint, paper, panel, etc.): ....

....

Total square footage of walls ....

Paint/covering used

Brand & color ....

Amount needed & cost ....

Purchased from .... Date ....

TRIM

Type of baseboard trim .... linear feet ....

Type of ceiling trim .... linear feet ....

Type of window trim .... linear feet ....

Type of door trim.. linear feet ....

Paint used

Brand & color..

Amount needed & cost...

Purchased from.. Date...................................

Contractor & contact details ....

....

Cost of work.. Date completed..........................

Warranty details ....

CEILING

Description of ceiling (paint, textured, etc.): ....

....

Total square footage of ceiling ....

Paint/covering used

Brand & color...

Amount needed & cost...

Purchased from .... Date ....

FLOORING

Total square footage of floor ....

Description of flooring (wood, carpet, tile, etc.): ....

....

Covering used

Brand & color...

Amount needed & cost...

Purchased from .... Date ....

Notes ....

....

Contractor & contact details ....

....

Cost of work .... Date completed ....

Warranty details...

WINDOWS AND DOORS

Type & material ....

Manufacturer & model ....

Size & number .... Cost ....

Purchased from .... Date ....

Notes ....

Installation company & contact information ....

Cost of work .... Date completed ....

Warranty details ....

WINDOW TREATMENTS

Description (blinds, curtains, etc.) & size ....

Brand & model ....

Color & number .... Cost ....

Purchased from .... Date ....

Notes ....

Installation company & contact information ....

Cost of work .... Date completed ....

Warranty details ....

LIGHT FIXTURES

Description (ceiling dome, recessed, free-standing, etc.) ....

....

....

Brand & model... Cost ....

Brand & model... Cost............................

Brand & model... Cost ....

Purchased from... Date ....

Notes on bulbs & control switches ....

....

Installation company & contact information ....

....

Cost of work.. Date completed ....

Warranty details...

INSPECTION & MAINTENANCE LOG

DATE   TASK   NOTES

....

....

....

....

....

....

OTHER ROOM 2

WALLS

Description of walls (paint, paper, panel, etc.): ....

....

Total square footage of walls ....

Paint/covering used

Brand & color ....

Amount needed & cost ....

Purchased from .... Date ....

TRIM

Type of baseboard trim .... linear feet ....

Type of ceiling trim .... linear feet ....

Type of window trim .... linear feet ....

Type of door trim.. linear feet ....

Paint used

Brand & color..

Amount needed & cost...

Purchased from.. Date............................

    Contractor & contact details ....

    ....

    Cost of work.. Date completed.....................

    Warranty details ....

CEILING

Description of ceiling (paint, textured, etc.): _____

_____

Total square footage of ceiling _____

Paint/covering used

Brand & color _____

Amount needed & cost _____

Purchased from _____ Date _____

FLOORING

Total square footage of floor _____

Description of flooring (wood, carpet, tile, etc.): _____

_____

Covering used

Brand & color _____

Amount needed & cost _____

Purchased from _____ Date _____

Notes _____

_____

Contractor & contact details _____

_____

Cost of work _____ Date completed _____

Warranty details _____

WINDOWS AND DOORS

Type & material ....

Manufacturer & model ....

Size & number.. Cost ....

Purchased from.. Date ....

Notes ....

Installation company & contact information ....

....

Cost of work.. Date completed ....

Warranty details ....

WINDOW TREATMENTS

Description (blinds, curtains, etc.) & size ....

....

Brand & model ....

Color & number.. Cost ....

Purchased from.. Date ....

Notes ....

Installation company & contact information ....

....

Cost of work.. Date completed ....

Warranty details ....

LIGHT FIXTURES

Description (ceiling dome, recessed, free-standing, etc.) ....

....

Brand & model... Cost ....

Brand & model... Cost ....

Brand & model... Cost ....

Purchased from... Date ....

Notes on bulbs & control switches ....

....

Installation company & contact information ....

....

Cost of work.. Date completed ....

Warranty details..

INSPECTION & MAINTENANCE LOG

DATE	TASK	NOTES

CLOSET RECORD

ROOM	CLOSET TYPE (WALK-IN, WALL, UTILITY, ETC.)	NOTES

VALUABLES

Use the following pages to keep track of your possessions for insurance purposes. Remember to use pencil or an erasable pen so the information contained in this chapter can be easily changed later.

APPLIANCE LOG

Note: For long-term appliance fixtures (water and HVAC systems), please refer to the end of the My Home chapter in the front.

ITEM	BRAND/MODEL/SERIAL #	PURCHASED (FROM/COST)	CONTACT INFO
REFRIGERATOR			
FREEZER			
STOVE/RANGE/OVEN			
TOASTER OVEN			
MICROWAVE			
DISHWASHER			
GARBAGE DISPOSAL			
TRASH COMPACTOR			
COFFEE MAKER			
BLENDER/JUICER			
WASHING MACHINE			
DRYER			
WALL/WINDOW AC			
WALL/WINDOW AC			
WALL/WINDOW AC			
VACUUM CLEANER			
SEWING MACHINE			
DEHUMIDIFIER			
AIR PURIFIER			
GENERATOR			

ELECTRONICS LOG

ITEM	BRAND/MODEL/SERIAL #	PURCHASED (FROM/COST)	CONTACT INFO
TELEVISION 1			
TELEVISION 2			
TELEVISION 3			
ENTERTAINMENT SYSTEM			
SPEAKERS			
DVD PLAYER			
STEREO			
CAMERA			
VIDEO CAMERA			
ROUTER			
GAME CONSOLE 1			
GAME CONSOLE 2			
COMPUTER 1			
COMPUTER 2			
COMPUTER 3			
PRINTER			
SCANNER			
OTHER			
OTHER			
OTHER			

FURNITURE LOG

ITEM	BRAND/MODEL/SERIAL #	PURCHASED (FROM/COST)	CONTACT INFO
BEDS			
NIGHTSTANDS			
END/ACCENT TABLES			
DINING TABLE			
HUTCH			
KITCHEN TABLE			
COFFEE TABLES			
CHAIRS			

ITEM	BRAND/MODEL/SERIAL #	PURCHASED (FROM/COST)	CONTACT INFO
RECLINERS			
SOFAS			
LOVESEATS			
OTTOMANS			
DESKS			
BOOKCASES			

ITEM	BRAND/MODEL/ SERIAL #	PURCHASED (FROM/COST)	CONTACT INFO
SHELVES			
DRESSERS/ CHESTS			
ARMOIRES			
MIRRORS			
FILE CABINETS			

VALUABLES LOG

ITEM	DESCRIPTION	SOURCE/DATE ACQUIRED	COST/VALUE ($)
JEWELRY			
ART			
VINYL RECORDS			
OTHER COLLECTIBLES			

ITEM	DESCRIPTION	SOURCE/DATE ACQUIRED	COST/VALUE ($)
CRYSTAL			
CHINA			
SILVERWARE			
VALUABLE CLOTHING			
WINE			
MUSICAL INSTRUMENTS			

ITEM	DESCRIPTION	SOURCE/DATE ACQUIRED	COST/VALUE ($)
CHANDELIERS			
EXERCISE EQUIPMENT			
LAWN MOWER			
STRING TRIMMER			
POWER TOOL SET			
HAND TOOL SET			
OTHER			

INSPECTIONS/ MAINTENANCE

U se the following pages to record yearly house inspections as well as any maintenance in between.

WHAT TO DO WHEN

Every 1–6 Months

Clean or change air filters for heating and cooling systems to keep them running as efficiently and economically as possible. (Note: Frequency depends on a number of factors, including how many people live in your home, whether or not you have pets, and if anyone living with you has allergies. The more people and pets living in your home, the more frequently you should be checking your air filters.)

Every 6 Months

Clean stove vent filter.

Clean humidifiers and dehumidifiers (during the seasons you use them).

Check water heater for signs of leaks or rust. Hot water tanks should be replaced every 10 years.

Every Year

Inspect foundation and basement for signs of termite infestation. Remove dense vegetation growing close to the foundation or siding.

Have furnace serviced.

If you use a fireplace, have the chimney cleaned and inspected.

Lubricate window hardware.

Inspect tile in bathrooms and kitchens. Loose tiles and grout need to be re-cemented and resealed.

Check floors for wear and damage, particularly where one material meets another.

Check electrical cords and overhead wiring, and replace at first sign of wear or damage.

Flush water heater.

Change batteries in smoke detectors. Check fire extinguishers to ensure they're fully charged.

Inspect area around septic tank for moist ground, sulfuric smell, or lush vegetation. Empty or replace tank as necessary.

Inspect gas shut-off valve.

Inspect porches and decks for warped ceilings or floors and damaged steps. Check for loose or rotten posts.

Look for animal nests on outside walls, fixtures, and eaves. Remove any you find or call a pest control professional.

Every Five Years

■ Have your home inspected by a professional inspector.

Every Spring and Autumn

■ Check doors, windows, and trim. Replace broken glass or damaged screens, and repair loose putty, caulking, and weather stripping.

■ Clean out gutters.

■ Inspect exterior walls, looking for cracks, paint failure, and damage to siding and trim.

■ Check fences, retaining walls, and stone walls for damage or warping.

■ Check roof for loose shingles. Check underside of roof for water stains or dampness.

■ Test ground-fault circuit breakers that are required for any area where there is water, such as kitchens and bathrooms.

■ Vacuum air ducts. Clean dryer ducts and vents.

■ Clean dirt and dust from around furnace.

■ Check driveways and sidewalks for cracks and yard for settlement and soil erosion. Fill in any low spots near the foundation with soil to prevent basement leaks.

■ Examine your trees and shrubs and prune back those that are too close to the house. Remove dead trees and broken limbs. Rake and remove or mulch leaves.

■ Check basement or crawl space for dampness and/or leakage following storms or heavy rains. Check sump pump.

■ Test smoke detectors and carbon monoxide detectors.

Before Winter

■ Remove window air conditioners or install insulated covers.

■ Shut off and drain outside water lines and hoses so water doesn't freeze.

■ Check radiators for leaks/clean radiators.

INSPECTION LOG

While running through the checklist on the previous pages, write down notes on actions taken and planned.

DATE	PART OF HOME INSPECTED	CONDITION/ NOTES

DATE	PART OF HOME INSPECTED	CONDITION/ NOTES

DATE	PART OF HOME INSPECTED	CONDITION/ NOTES

DATE	PART OF HOME INSPECTED	CONDITION/ NOTES

REMODELING

Need a change of scenery? The following pages will help you plan big projects and customize your house exactly as you'd like it. Use the grid paper to map out your house and play with layouts, then use the charts at the end of the chapter to take notes on what tasks you'll need to do to make your dream house a reality.

LANDSCAPING MAP

ATTIC

BASEMENT/CELLAR

KITCHEN/PANTRY

DINING ROOM

LIVING ROOM

FAMILY/RECREATION ROOM

BEDROOM 1

BEDROOM 2

BEDROOM 3

BEDROOM/SPARE ROOM

BATHROOM 1

BATHROOM 2

BATHROOM 3

LAUNDRY ROOM

ENTRY

HALL/STAIRS 1

HALL/STAIRS 2

OTHER ROOM 1

REMODELING NOTES

Jot down ideas and to-do items for remodeling projects in the chart below.

DATE	LOCATION	TASK/NOTES

DATE	LOCATION	TASK/NOTES

NOTES

NOTES

NOTES